EYEWITNESS TO HISTORY

MALCOLM X

in his own words

Gareth Stevens
PUBLISHING

By Sarah Machajewski

Please visit our website, www.garethstevens.com. For a free color catalog of all our high-quality books, call toll free 1-800-542-2595 or fax 1-877-542-2596.

Library of Congress Cataloging-in-Publication Data

Machajewski, Sarah.
Malcolm X in his own words / by Sarah Machajewski.
p. cm. — (Eyewitness to history)
Includes index.
ISBN 978-1-4824-1281-9 (pbk.)
ISBN 978-1-4824-1220-8 (6-pack)
ISBN 978-1-4824-1481-3 (library binding)
1. X, Malcolm, — 1925-1965 — Juvenile literature. 2. Black Muslims — Biography — Juvenile literature. 3. African Americans — Biography — Juvenile literature. I. Machajewski, Sarah. II. Title.
BP223.Z8 M33 2015
320.54—d23

First Edition

Published in 2015 by
Gareth Stevens Publishing
111 East 14th Street, Suite 349
New York, NY 10003

Copyright © 2015 Gareth Stevens Publishing

Designer: Katelyn E. Reynolds
Editor: Therese Shea

Photo credits: Cover, p. 1 (Malcolm X) Bob Parent/Hulton Archive/Getty Images; cover, p. 1 (background image) Hulton Archive/Getty Images; cover, p. 1 (logo quill icon) Seamartini Graphics Media/Shutterstock.com; cover, p. 1 (logo stamp) YasnaTen/Shutterstock.com; cover, p. 1 (color grunge frame) DmitryPrudnichenko/ Shutterstock.com; cover, pp. 1–32 (paper background) Nella/Shutterstock.com; cover, pp. 1–32 (decorative elements) Ozerina Anna/Shutterstock.com; pp. 1–32 (wood texture) Reinhold Leitner/Shutterstock.com; pp. 1–32 (open book background) Elena Schweitzer/Shutterstock.com; pp. 1–32 (bookmark) Robert Adrian Hillman/ Shutterstock.com; pp. 4–5 Buyenlarge/Getty Images; p. 7 MPI/Getty Images; p. 9 U.S. Library of Congress, George Grantham Bain Collection/Wikipedia.com; p. 11 (signature) Connormah/Wikipedia.com; pp. 11 (image), 19 courtesy of the Library of Congress; p. 13 Truman Moore/Time Life Pictures/Getty Images; pp. 14–15 Richard Saunders/ Pictorial Parade/Archive Photos/Getty Images; p. 17 Marvin Lichtner/Time Life Pictures/ Getty Images; pp. 21, 23 Burt Shavitz/Pix Inc/Time Life Pictures/Getty Images; p. 25 Robert Parent/Time Life Pictures/Getty Images; p. 27 Pictorial Parade/Archive Photos/ Getty Images; p. 28 NY Daily News Archive/Getty Images.

Printed in the United States of America

CPSIA compliance information: Batch #CS15GS: For further information contact Gareth Stevens, New York, New York at 1-800-542-2595.

CONTENTS

A Time of Change 4

Growing Up in Racist America 6

A Prison Education 8

Becoming "X" 10

Growing the Nation 12

The Hate That Hate Produced 16

Malcolm X and MLK 18

"By Any Means Necessary" 20

Freedom, Justice, Equality 22

The Chickens Come Home to Roost 24

A Change of Heart 26

Malcolm's Legacy 28

Glossary 30

For More Information 31

Index 32

*Words in the glossary appear in **bold** type the first time they are used in the text.*

A TIME
of Change

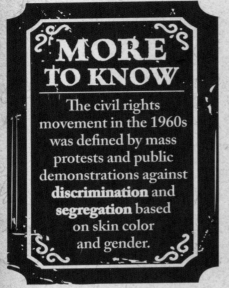

MORE TO KNOW

The civil rights movement in the 1960s was defined by mass protests and public demonstrations against **discrimination** and **segregation** based on skin color and gender.

The 1960s in the United States were a time of great social change. Many Americans were tired of the way society and the government treated them. African Americans were one group whose fight for equality defined this decade.

Though slavery was abolished in the United States in 1865, African Americans continued to experience social injustices and unequal treatment. Violence and **racism** against them still occurred, and many had to attend separate schools and use different public facilities that were often poorly maintained and supplied.

One hundred years after slavery, many African Americans felt they had had enough. In the fight for **civil rights**, certain figures

4

emerged as leaders because of their ideas about how to gain equality and justice. Malcolm X was one of them.

People peacefully march to end Jim Crow laws, which made the segregation of blacks and whites legal in the South.

HISTORY IN HIS OWN WORDS

Malcolm X became a notable historical leader thanks to his **unique** system of beliefs and ideas. The best way to understand his viewpoints is to read his own words. This book uses primary sources to do just that.

Primary sources are materials created by somebody who was present during a time of history. They include letters, speeches, and interviews. They give us an inside look at a particular event, moment, or period of time.

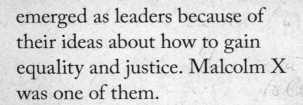

5

GROWING UP
in Racist America

SHATTERED DREAMS

Malcolm X was very smart. He was at the top of his class in junior high and had dreams of becoming a lawyer. However, when he shared this dream with his favorite teacher, Mr. Ostrowski, his teacher said it was *"no realistic goal"* because he was black. The comment led Malcolm to lose interest in school. It was this kind of racism that African Americans would fight against in the 1960s.

Though the world knows him as Malcolm X, he was born Malcolm Little on May 19, 1925, in Omaha, Nebraska. His parents followed the teachings of Marcus Garvey, a political leader who believed in Black Nationalism, a movement that supported a separate black society. These beliefs brought unwelcome attention to their family. In 1929, the Littles' home was burned down. Two years later, Malcolm's father died in an accident. Malcolm believed his father was murdered. Malcolm's mother became mentally ill. The eight Little children were sent to foster homes and orphanages.

Malcolm went to Boston in 1941 to live with his sister Ella. In his **autobiography**, he said, *"No physical move in my life has ever been more pivotal or profound in its **repercussions**."*

6

A difficult childhood put Malcolm on the wrong path at first. He dropped out of school following the eighth grade, after one of his teachers told him becoming a lawyer wasn't "realistic."

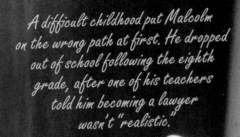

7

A PRISON *Education*

MORE TO KNOW

The Nation of Islam is a religious organization that combines teachings of Islam and the Black Nationalism movement. Nation members believe in Allah, the Islamic name for God, and follow traditional Islamic teachings such as refusing to eat pork or to use tobacco and alcohol.

After working various jobs, Malcolm began a life of crime in New York City and Boston. In 1946, he was arrested in Massachusetts and sentenced to 8 to 10 years in prison. This was a turning point in Malcolm's life. He said prison was the *"greatest thing that ever happened"* to him because it was there that he learned about the Nation of Islam, changing the course of his life forever.

Malcolm spent long hours studying the teachings of the Nation of Islam's leader, Elijah Muhammad. Malcolm told a magazine in 1963 that he was *"nothing but another convict, a semi-illiterate criminal . . . [the teachings] were able to reach into prison, which is the level where people are considered to have fallen as low as they can go."* The Nation of Islam gave him a chance for another life.

8

Marcus Garvey (1887–1940) urged African Americans to take pride in their race. He created the "Back to Africa" movement.

A SEPARATE SOCIETY

Malcolm's parents believed in Black Nationalism, and later, he did, too. Black Nationalism was an idea made popular by Marcus Garvey in the 1920s. The movement taught that blacks should be proud of their heritage and preached that they could have their own independent society separate from whites. African Americans could support themselves economically by running their own businesses. Elijah Muhammad even wanted a separate black nation using land in Georgia, Alabama, and Mississippi.

9

BECOMING "X"

MORE TO KNOW

In Malcolm's autobiography, he said, *"For me, my X" replaced the white slavemaster name of 'Little'...imposed on my paternal forebearers."*

Malcolm's conversion to the Nation of Islam involved giving up something that had defined his public identity: his last name. This was a custom among Nation members who believed their last names came from the white people who enslaved their ancestors. In a TV interview, Malcolm said, *"During slavery, the same slavemaster who owned us put his last name on us to* **denote** *that we were his property."*

Malcolm replaced his last name with the letter "X." When pressed by the TV host to tell him his father's last name, Malcolm stuck to his beliefs: *"The last name of my forefathers was taken from them when they were brought to America and made slaves . . . We reject that [slave] name today and refuse it . . . I never acknowledge it whatsoever."*

10

Malcolm's actual signature:

Malcolm X

Malcolm started going by Malcolm X as early as 1950.

WHAT'S IN A NAME?

Malcolm chose "X" as his last name because he never knew his African ancestors' names. The X represented that unknown and the loss of identity experienced coming to the United States as slaves. Malcolm used X in all areas of his life, including when he married his wife, Betty, in 1958. She took the name Betty X. Later, they changed their last name again when Malcolm adopted a new set of Islamic beliefs.

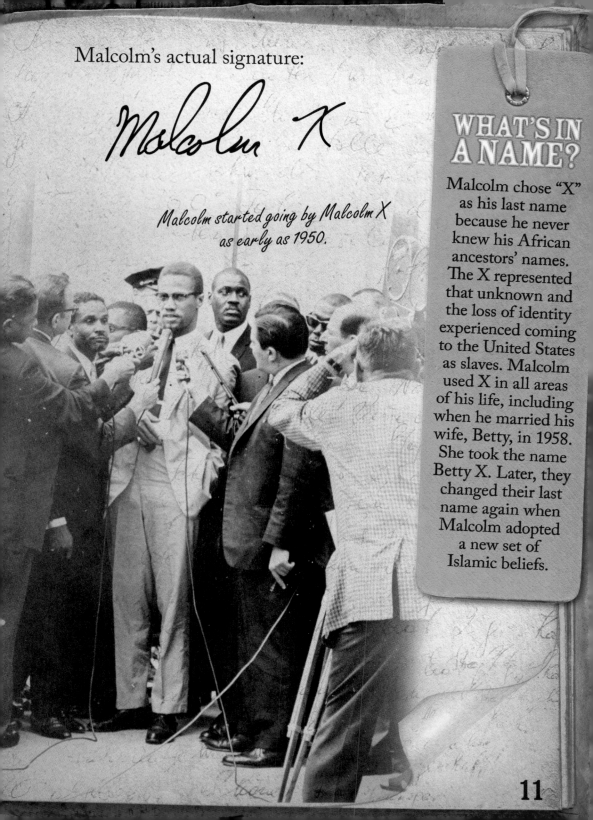

11

GROWING
the Nation

THE HONORABLE ELIJAH MUHAMMAD

Malcolm was very inspired by the Nation's teachings. In a 1955 letter to his sister, Malcolm wrote that the Nation's teachings were the *"truth"* and that they *"open your eyes to different things around you."* The Nation of Islam was special to Malcolm since it gave him a purpose in life and something to believe in. He felt it could do the same for others and set out to grow the Nation's membership.

Malcolm came to the Nation of Islam at a fitting time. The American civil rights movement was just beginning, and signs were showing that black Americans were through with the unfair treatment they had always experienced. Black leaders with different **ideologies** started getting attention for their approaches to gaining equality. Soon, Malcolm would be included among them.

Malcolm's mentor, Elijah Muhammad, led the Nation of Islam from the 1930s until he died in 1975. He was known for his extreme viewpoints, especially the angry way he talked about white people. He wanted blacks to be completely separate from white society. He also preached violence as a means of self-defense. Many people viewed him as racist. Malcolm's dedication to Elijah Muhammad caused some to fear him and others to admire him.

12

MORE TO KNOW

Malcolm became the assistant minister of Detroit's Nation of Islam Temple No. 1 soon after he moved there. In 1954, he became the minister of Temple No. 7 in Harlem, which he led for almost 10 years.

Malcolm organized temples for the Nation of Islam in New York, Philadelphia, and Boston and in cities in the South. He also founded the Nation's newspaper, Muhammad Speaks.

13

Elijah Muhammad quickly realized Malcolm's intelligence and gift for public speaking. He appointed him to be the Nation of Islam's national spokesman. Malcolm's commitment to the Nation and his way of communicating its ideas attracted many new members. The Nation of Islam grew from 500 members in 1952 to over 30,000 by 1963.

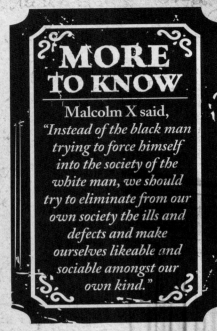

People paid attention to Malcolm because he expressed the anger, struggle, and thirst for freedom felt by African Americans for decades—and he didn't apologize for it. *"Just as the white man and every other person on this earth has God-given rights, natural rights, civil rights, any kind of right that you can think of when it comes to defending himself,"* he said, *"black people should have the right to defend ourselves also."*

14

Large numbers of people flocked to Nation of Islam rallies to hear Malcolm X speak.

BLACK AND WHITE VIEWS

Many black leaders of the civil rights movement felt that the goal should be total **integration** between whites and blacks. However, Malcolm and Black Muslims (as Nation members were sometimes called) wanted nothing to do with integration; they didn't want to live peacefully among the people who, they believed, had enslaved them and been racist toward them. *"Complete separation is the only solution to the black and white problem in this country,"* Malcolm said.

15

THE HATE
That Hate Produced

A BIASED VIEW

The Hate That Hate Produced aired from July 13 to July 17, 1959. The documentary included untrue statements, inaccuracies, and opinions that intentionally made the Nation seem racist, hateful, and scary. Most white viewers were alarmed at what they saw. For many people, it was their first time ever learning about this small group of people within the civil rights movement. Up until that time, the movement was known mostly for its message of nonviolence and **civil disobedience**.

Malcolm spent several years working to grow the Nation of Islam's membership. He traveled to different areas and used TV and radio to spread his message. However, none of these efforts were as effective in drawing attention to the Nation as a **documentary** called *The Hate That Hate Produced*.

The 1959 television program was produced by two news reporters and featured interviews with several of the organization's high-ranking officials, including Malcolm X. Malcolm was shown in the documentary saying that *"by nature [the white man] is evil."*

Viewers, both white and black, were shocked at what they saw. The Nation of Islam came to be known as a hate

16

group that was racist towards whites. Their beliefs and angry speeches created a division between them and other civil rights activists who preached nonviolence.

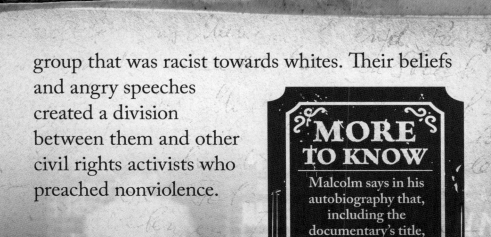

MORE TO KNOW

Malcolm says in his autobiography that, including the documentary's title, *"every phrase was edited to increase the shock mood."*

The Nation of Islam and Malcolm X helped change terms used to refer to African Americans from "Negro" and "colored" to "black" and "African American."

17

MALCOLM X
and MLK

Malcolm gained a lot of attention because of how different his ideas were from those of other black leaders within the civil rights movement, especially Martin Luther King Jr. Malcolm was often

MORE TO KNOW

Martin Luther King Jr. once wrote to Malcolm's wife: *"No one can honestly doubt that Malcolm had a great concern for the problems we face as a race."*

asked for his opinions on King's ideology. He thought King's nonviolent approach was too weak in such a racist world.

King called on whites and blacks to live peacefully together, but in Malcolm's view, King's goal was to get blacks *"to forgive the people who have brutalized them for 400 years and . . . [make] them forget what those whites have done to them."*

The leaders' differing views caused many people to compare their successes and failures. Over time, the two men have become symbols of the two ideologies that defined the civil rights movement.

18

Though they held opposing beliefs, Malcolm X and Martin Luther King Jr. are both known as heroes of the civil rights movement.

"A COMMON SOLUTION"

Malcolm's methods were very different from King's and other African American leaders'. But ultimately their goals were the same: gaining equality. In 1963, Malcolm wrote to King and other leaders inviting them to come together as a united front: *"it is a disgrace for Negro leaders to not be able to submerge our 'minor' differences in order to seek a common solution to a common problem."*

19

"BY ANY *Means Necessary*"

The media quickly took notice of Malcolm X and his views on the problems of race in America. He used the media's interest as an opportunity to spread his ideology to the masses.

Malcolm gave many memorable speeches. In one of his most famous, he said, *"We declare our right . . . to be a human being, to be respected as a human being, to be given the rights of a human being . . . which we intend to bring into existence by any means necessary."* The means he talked about referred to everything—including violence. The phrase *"by any means necessary"* has become forever attached to Malcolm X's message. Malcolm made it clear that he didn't think civil disobedience was effective, especially for self-defense.

SELF-DEFENSE

Malcolm X became associated with a message of violence, but it's more correct to say he preached self-defense. He never said African Americans should start violence, but he did say they should use it to defend themselves when people were violent toward them. In a 1964 interview with the magazine *Monthly Review*, he said, *"We have never initiated violence against anyone, but we do believe that when violence is practiced against us we should be able to defend ourselves."*

20

MORE TO KNOW

Malcolm's message led many people to view him as a **militant**. However, when once asked by an interviewer if he considered himself to be, Malcolm laughed and said, *"I consider myself Malcolm."*

This photo is one of the most famous images of Malcolm X. With his hand raised, he looks powerful and determined.

FREEDOM,
Justice, Equality

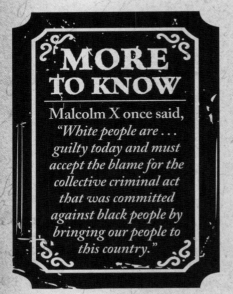

MORE TO KNOW

Malcolm X once said, *"White people are . . . guilty today and must accept the blame for the collective criminal act that was committed against black people by bringing our people to this country."*

The attention on the Nation of Islam thrust Malcolm even more into the public eye. Because he was the spokesperson for a group that was seen as racist and antiwhite, many people labeled Malcolm as that, too.

At a rally in New York in 1964, he declared, *"They've always said that I'm antiwhite. I'm for anybody who's for freedom. I'm for anybody who's for justice. I'm for anybody who's for equality. . . . I'm not for anybody who tells black people to be nonviolent while nobody is telling white people to be nonviolent."*

Malcolm said he wasn't antiwhite. In fact, he said, *"I believe that there are some white people who might be sincere. But I think they should prove it."* He wanted them to fight for black rights, too.

22

Malcolm's intelligence and wit made him a popular speaker at many places, from rallies on city streets to Harvard University.

FIERY LANGUAGE

People saw Malcolm as racist because he pointed the finger at white people for the problems African Americans faced. He blamed whites for bringing blacks to America as slaves, for letting slavery exist, and then for having social, political, and economic systems that kept them unequal. When people heard his words, they couldn't help but view him as antiwhite.

23

THE CHICKENS
Come Home to Roost

KENNEDY AND CIVIL RIGHTS

Though Malcolm said President Kennedy failed to stop violence against blacks, the president did play an important role in the civil rights movement until his death in 1963. He appointed several African Americans to important positions within his administration and supported the desegregation of schools. When the University of Alabama tried to keep black students from enrolling, Kennedy sent the National Guard to force the school to integrate. Kennedy died before he could pass any civil rights laws.

Malcolm's words both inspired and scared people. He went too far in late 1963, according to the Nation of Islam. In talking about the assassination, or killing, of President John F. Kennedy, Malcolm said, *"I think this is a prime example of the devil's chickens coming back home to roost."* He meant that Kennedy had failed to stop violence against blacks, so the violence came back and was committed against him.

People were shocked and offended by Malcolm's words. He said he meant the president's assassination was *"a result of the climate of hate."* Regardless, the Nation of Islam was embarrassed, and Elijah Muhammad ordered Malcolm

24

to stay silent for 90 days. Eventually, Malcolm left after disagreeing with Muhammad's actions as a leader and the direction of the organization.

Malcolm X had wanted the Nation of Islam to become more active in civil rights protests. This was just one of his disagreements with the Nation and Elijah Muhammad's leadership.

25

A CHANGE
of Heart

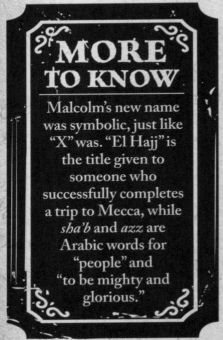

MORE TO KNOW

Malcolm's new name was symbolic, just like "X" was. "El Hajj" is the title given to someone who successfully completes a trip to Mecca, while *sha'b* and *azz* are Arabic words for "people" and "to be mighty and glorious."

Leaving the Nation of Islam was a turning point in Malcolm's life. Without the organization, he had to find a new way to express his faith and beliefs. He founded Muslim Mosque, Inc., his own version of a black Islamist organization.

That same year, Malcolm traveled to Mecca, the holy Muslim city located in Saudi Arabia. He had a spiritual awakening when he saw Muslims of all races, including white, worshipping together. He had met *"blonde-haired, blue-eyed men I could call my brothers."* He returned to the United States with new hope for integration and changed his name to El-Hajj Malik el-Shabazz. Malcolm told a group of students in 1964 that *"the most important thing we can learn to do today is think for ourselves."*

26

Malcolm X arrives in New York City after his life-transforming tour of the Middle East in May 1964.

AFRO-AMERICAN UNITY

Malcolm's trip to Mecca changed everything. He always believed in black separatism, but he now felt he could work with other races. His activist efforts had previously only focused on civil rights, but now he wanted to focus on human rights, too. He founded the Organization of Afro-American Unity in 1965. It was a nonreligious group that joined the cause of black Americans with Africans around the world.

27

MALCOLM'S *Legacy*

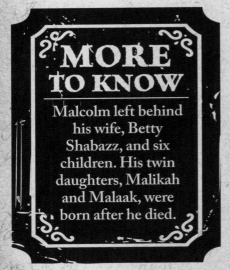

MORE TO KNOW

Malcolm left behind his wife, Betty Shabazz, and six children. His twin daughters, Malikah and Malaak, were born after he died.

Malcolm received several death threats after he broke from the Nation of Islam. There was tension between him and Nation members because of their differences. Nation members plotted to plant a bomb in Malcolm's car, and his home was firebombed on February 14, 1964. On February 21, 1965, three Nation members stormed a lecture he was giving at the Audubon Ballroom in New York City and shot him. He was only 39 years old when he died.

Malcolm's words brought the plight of African Americans to national attention and refused to let people look away. Today, we remember Malcolm as a leader who inspired oppressed people to demand justice.

28

TIMELINE
THE LIFE OF MALCOLM X

1925 — Malcolm Little born May 19 in Omaha, Nebraska

1929 — Little home burned down, possibly by white racists

1931 — Malcolm's father dies in accident

1941 — Malcolm moves to Boston, Massachusetts, to live with his sister

1946 — Malcolm is arrested and imprisoned; joins Nation of Islam

ca. 1950 — Malcolm drops his last name and goes by "Malcolm X"

1952 — Malcolm released from prison and moves to Detroit, Michigan; meets Elijah Muhammad, the Nation's leader

1954 — Malcolm becomes minister of the Nation's Temple No. 7 in Harlem

1959 — documentary *The Hate That Hate Produced* airs

1963 — Malcolm comments about President Kennedy's assassination and is "silenced" by Nation of Islam

March 1964 — Malcolm breaks from Nation of Islam; founds Muslim Mosque, Inc.

1964 — Malcolm journeys to Mecca; changes his name to El-Hajj Malik el-Shabazz

1965 — Malcolm X assassinated on February 21 during a lecture in New York City

"MEANINGFUL TRUTH"

Malcolm had worked with writer Alex Haley on his autobiography since 1963. It was completed after his death. The text closes with Malcolm stating it was all thanks to Allah *"if I can die having brought any light, having exposed any meaningful truth that will help to destroy the racist cancer . . . in the body of America."* His autobiography became a national bestseller and is read today to understand the complicated man still widely remembered as Malcolm X.

29

GLOSSARY

autobiography: a book written by someone about their life

civil disobedience: the breaking of a law as a form of nonviolent protest to force change

civil rights: the personal freedoms granted to US citizens by law

denote: to be a sign or representation of something

discrimination: unfairly treating people unequally because of their race or beliefs

documentary: a movie or TV program presenting information about an issue

ideology: a set of beliefs, values, and ideas that shape an individual

integration: the act or process of opening a group, community, or place to all people

militant: a person who will use force to support a cause or belief

profound: extending to great lengths

racism: the belief that people of different races have different qualities and abilities and that some are superior or inferior

repercussion: something that results from an action

segregation: the forced separation of races or classes

unique: one of a kind

FOR MORE
Information

Books

Shabazz, Ilyasah. *Malcolm Little: The Boy Who Grew Up to Become Malcolm X*. New York, NY: Atheneum Books for Young Readers, 2013.

X, Malcolm, and Alex Haley. *The Autobiography of Malcolm X*. New York, NY: Ballantine Books, 1992.

Websites

African American World
pbskids.org/aaworld/
PBS provides an interactive website dedicated to prominent African American leaders, including Malcolm X.

Malcolm X: Historical Photo Gallery
malcolmx.com/about/photos.html
See photos of Malcolm X on his official website.

INDEX

autobiography 6, 10, 17, 29

Betty 11, 28

Black Muslims 15

Black Nationalism 6, 8, 9

civil disobedience 16, 20

civil rights 4, 12, 14, 15, 16, 17, 18, 19, 24, 25, 27

death 28, 29

equality 4, 5, 12, 19, 22

Garvey, Marcus 6, 9

hate group 16

Hate That Hate Produced, The 16, 29

human rights 27

integration 15, 24, 26

justice 5, 22, 28

King, Martin Luther, Jr. 18, 19

Little, Malcolm 6, 10, 29

Muhammad, Elijah 8, 9, 12, 14, 24, 25, 29

Muslim Mosque, Inc. 26, 29

name change 10, 11, 26, 29

national spokesman 14, 22

Nation of Islam 8, 10, 12, 13, 14, 15, 16, 17, 22, 24, 25, 26, 28, 29

nonviolence 16, 17, 18, 22

Organization of Afro-American Unity 27

prison 8, 29

racism 4, 6, 12, 15, 16, 17, 18, 22, 23, 29

self-defense 12, 14, 20

slavery 4, 10, 11, 15, 23

Temple No. 7 13, 29

trip to Mecca 26, 27, 29

violence 4, 12, 20, 24